STEM

The Science of Travel

Multiplication

Kat Bernardo, M.Ed.

Consultants

Michele Ogden, Ed.D
Principal, Irvine Unified School District

Jennifer Robertson, M.A.Ed.
Teacher, Huntington Beach City School District

Publishing Credits

Rachelle Cracchiolo, M.S.Ed., *Publisher*
Conni Medina, M.A.Ed., *Managing Editor*
Dona Herweck Rice, *Series Developer*
Emily R. Smith, M.A.Ed., *Series Developer*
Diana Kenney, M.A.Ed., NBCT, *Content Director*
Stacy Monsman, M.A., *Editor*
Kevin Panter, *Graphic Designer*

Image Credits: p. 11 Julio Bulnes/Alamy Stock Photo; p.19 Illustration by Timothy J. Bradley; all other images from iStock and/or Shutterstock.

Library of Congress Cataloging-in-Publication Data

Names: Bernardo, Kat, author.
Title: STEM : the science of travel / Kat Bernardo.
Other titles: Science of travel
Description: Huntington Beach, CA : Teacher Created Materials, [2017] | Audience: K to grade 3. | Includes index.
Identifiers: LCCN 2016053555 (print) | LCCN 2017009869 (ebook) | ISBN 9781480757974 (pbk.) | ISBN 9781480758612 (eBook)
Subjects: LCSH: Travel--Juvenile literature. | Vacations--Juvenile literature. | Mathematics--Problems, exercises, etc.--Juvenile literature.
Classification: LCC G175 .B47 2017 (print) | LCC G175 (ebook) | DDC 910.2--dc23
LC record available at https://lccn.loc.gov/2016053555

Teacher Created Materials
5301 Oceanus Drive
Huntington Beach, CA 92649-1030
http://www.tcmpub.com

ISBN 978-1-4807-5797-4

Table of Contents

Note to the reader: The Hawaiian language includes a letter that looks like this: ‘. It is called an ‘okina. It signifies a stop between two sounds. Another Hawaiian mark is the kahakō and signifies a long vowel sound. For ease of reading, this story uses standard English spelling.

Let's Take a Trip!

Many people love to vacation with family. Luckily, you don't have to go far to have a good time. There are adventures close to home. You can spend the day visiting museums and parks right in your own neighborhood.

But what if you want to take a trip farther from home? Maybe you want to visit family and friends who live far away. Or, perhaps you want to see as many sights as you can in a new place.

No matter what you choose, you will probably need some sort of transportation to get you where you want to go. Whether in the air or on land, far away or in your own backyard, getting there can be part of the fun. Pack your bags and buckle up! It is time to take a family vacation!

Airplane to Hawaii

Shawn and Catie Burke are taking their first trip on an airplane. They are so excited! Their family is going on a vacation to Hawaii. They have their tickets, and a hotel room is waiting. The only thing left to do is fly!

The Burkes drive to the airport. Once there, they wheel their heavy bags to the gate agent. Because the bags are so big, they need to be stored in the cargo hold of the airplane. The agent sticks a special tag to their suitcases. Then, the agent places the bags on a long **conveyor belt** behind the desk. Shawn gets worried when he sees his bag roll out of sight. The agent tells him that the luggage tag has a bar code on it. A computer will scan the bar code. Then, workers will load the bag onto the correct airplane.

A family waits for an airport agent to tag their luggage.

LET'S EXPLORE MATH

Uh-oh! The gate agent is running behind. A lot of people came to the counter at the same time to check in. There are now 4 carts loaded with luggage waiting to be tagged. Each cart has 6 pieces of luggage.

1. How many pieces of luggage are there total?
2. The luggage belongs to 8 people. If each person brought the same number of bags, how many bags did each person bring?

A safety inspector checks X-rays of bags to keep everyone safe.

Four Forces

Before the Burkes can board the airplane, they need to go through security. Catie takes off her shoes. She places them on a conveyor belt with her small carry-on bag. The items move under a metal box as an agent inspects a screen. Catie sees an X-ray of her shoes and bag! The agent tells her that she checks to make sure people are following the rules. She wants to keep the airport safe.

The Burkes arrive at the gate and wait to board their plane. Shawn asks his dad how something so big can fly. His dad explains that it has to do with four **forces**. **Gravity** pulls the airplane toward the ground. **Lift** from the forward motion of the plane pushes it up. The lift of an airplane must be stronger than gravity for it to take off. **Drag** from the size and shape of the plane slows it down. But, **thrust** from the engines pushes the plane forward. The pilot makes sure the airplane's thrust is stronger than the drag. All four of these forces work together to keep the plane moving forward.

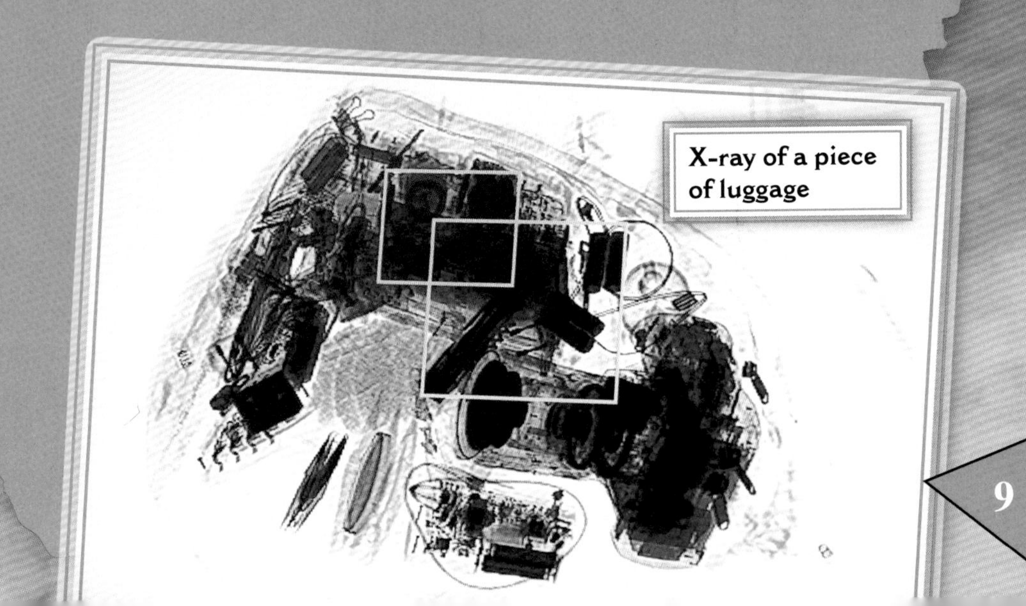
X-ray of a piece of luggage

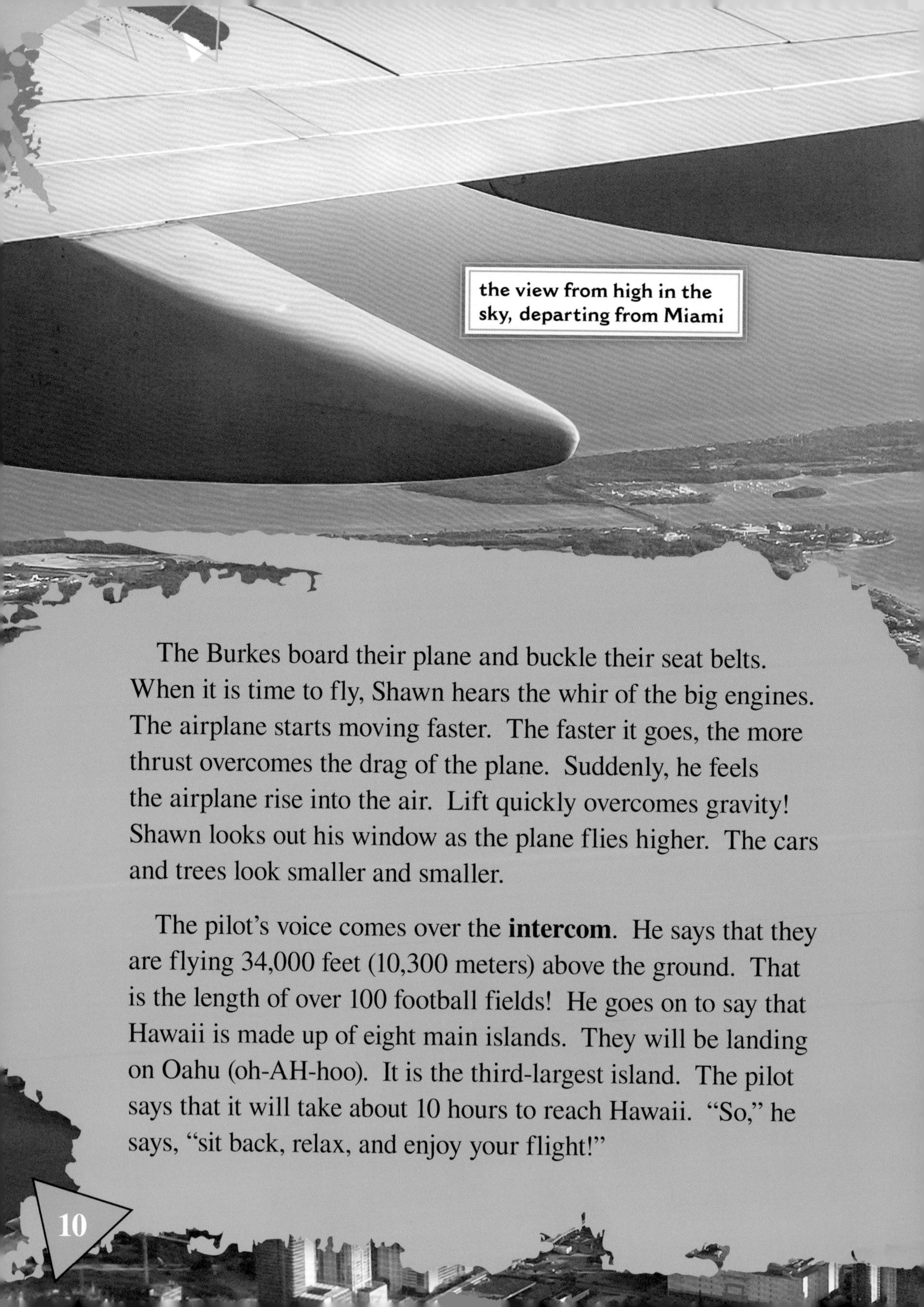

the view from high in the sky, departing from Miami

The Burkes board their plane and buckle their seat belts. When it is time to fly, Shawn hears the whir of the big engines. The airplane starts moving faster. The faster it goes, the more thrust overcomes the drag of the plane. Suddenly, he feels the airplane rise into the air. Lift quickly overcomes gravity! Shawn looks out his window as the plane flies higher. The cars and trees look smaller and smaller.

The pilot's voice comes over the **intercom**. He says that they are flying 34,000 feet (10,300 meters) above the ground. That is the length of over 100 football fields! He goes on to say that Hawaii is made up of eight main islands. They will be landing on Oahu (oh-AH-hoo). It is the third-largest island. The pilot says that it will take about 10 hours to reach Hawaii. "So," he says, "sit back, relax, and enjoy your flight!"

LET'S EXPLORE MATH

As the flight attendant walks down the aisle, he tells the passengers about the islands.

1. Niihau (nee-ee-HOW) is the seventh-largest Hawaiian island, so it is smaller than Oahu. At its widest point, Niihau is only 6 miles wide! Oahu is 5 times as wide as Niihau. How many miles wide is Oahu?
2. Oahu is 3 times as wide as the fifth-largest island, Molokai (moh-loh-KY). How many miles wide is Molokai?

Honolulu, Hawaii

Chopper over Oahu

When the Burkes land in Oahu, their uncle Andy greets them at the airport. He is a helicopter pilot. Today is a special day. Uncle Andy is taking Shawn and Catie on an **aerial** tour of the island! They can't wait to see the view from up high.

Andy shows Shawn and Catie how to climb into their seats. They put on big headphones to protect their ears from the noise. But these are not just any headphones. They are walkie-talkies! Shawn and Catie can hear Uncle Andy talking to them. He tells them that helicopters fly with the help of long **rotors**. These blades spin, or chop, the air. The spinning motion creates lift that pushes the chopper up. As they fly higher, the people and cars below look like ants. Soon, they are soaring 2,000 ft. (600 m) high!

Diamond Head

Catie looks down and sees a huge hole in the ground. Uncle Andy tells her that 300,000 years ago, a volcano erupted. Hot ash and tiny pieces of earth shot into the air. When they settled, Diamond Head crater was formed. Catie is amazed at the size of it. Shawn and Catie want to do more than see the crater from above. They want to hike to the top!

After their aerial tour, Uncle Andy drives them to the crater. Shawn jogs ahead to see the first glimpse of it up close. But the path is tough. It is a good thing they wore their sturdy hiking boots! They start up the side of the crater, climbing a series of **switchback** trails. Shawn is tired, but they have not reached the top yet. He looks ahead and sees a sign for the final 99 stairs. At last, they reach the top. They are now 760 ft. (230 m) above the ocean.

The sun is starting to set, and it is time to head back. Shawn, Catie, and Uncle Andy begin their trek back down the crater's side.

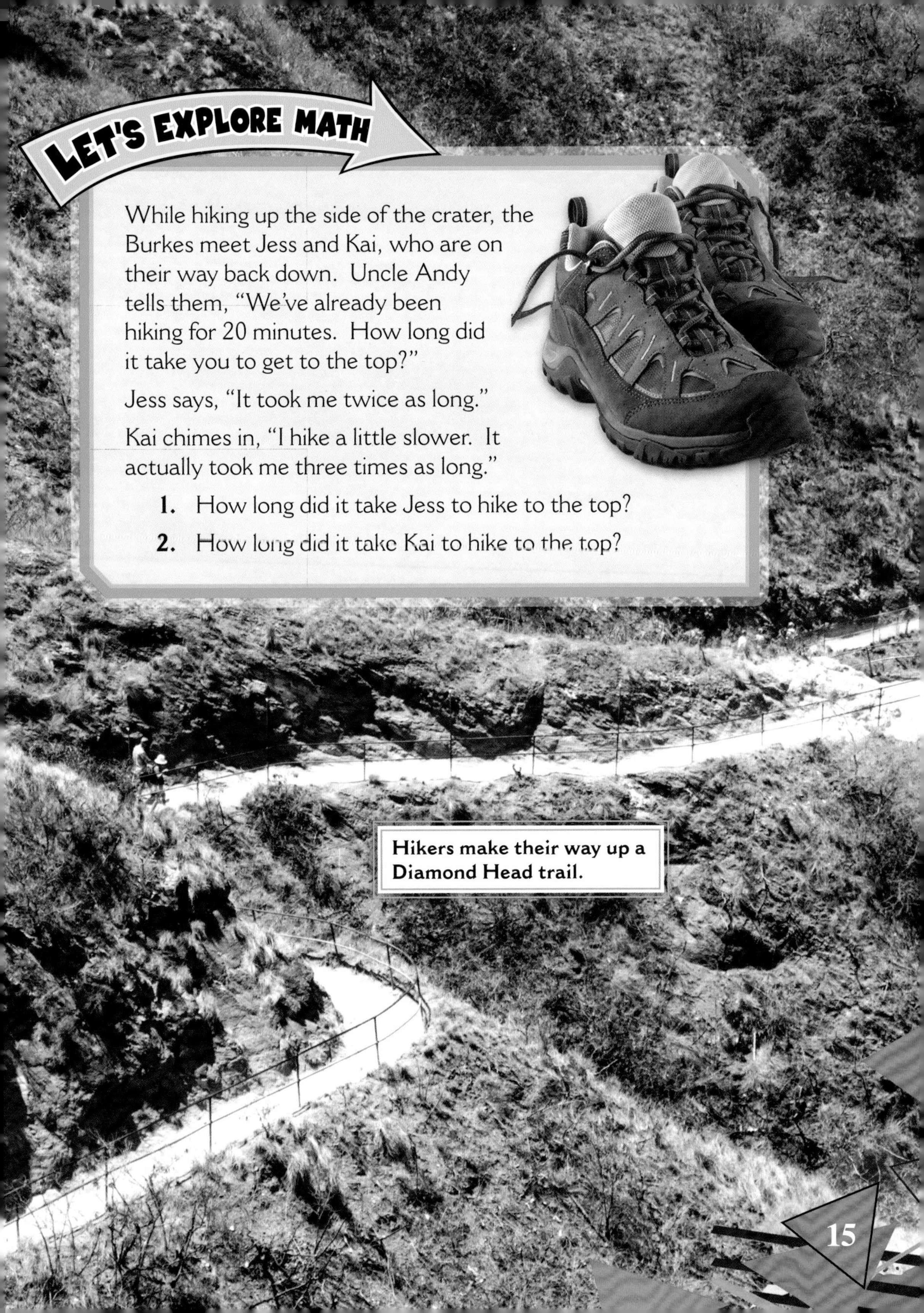

Let's Explore Math

While hiking up the side of the crater, the Burkes meet Jess and Kai, who are on their way back down. Uncle Andy tells them, "We've already been hiking for 20 minutes. How long did it take you to get to the top?"

Jess says, "It took me twice as long."

Kai chimes in, "I hike a little slower. It actually took me three times as long."

1. How long did it take Jess to hike to the top?
2. How long did it take Kai to hike to the top?

Hikers make their way up a Diamond Head trail.

Maglev in Motion

On the other side of the world, another family steps off an airplane. Sheng and Lin Liu have been waiting months for this day to come. The Lius just spent three hours on an airplane to Shanghai, China. They can't wait to visit their family! Plus, they can explore the city. Just one last trip, and they will be on their way!

The Lius head to baggage claim where they pick up their luggage. Lin spots a sign for the maglev train. *Maglev* is short for "magnetic **levitation**." This high-speed train is the fastest in the world! It will take them to Longyang Road Station near downtown Shanghai. Lin leads her family upstairs and out the front doors toward the train. She can't wait to see how fast it goes!

Shanghai maglev

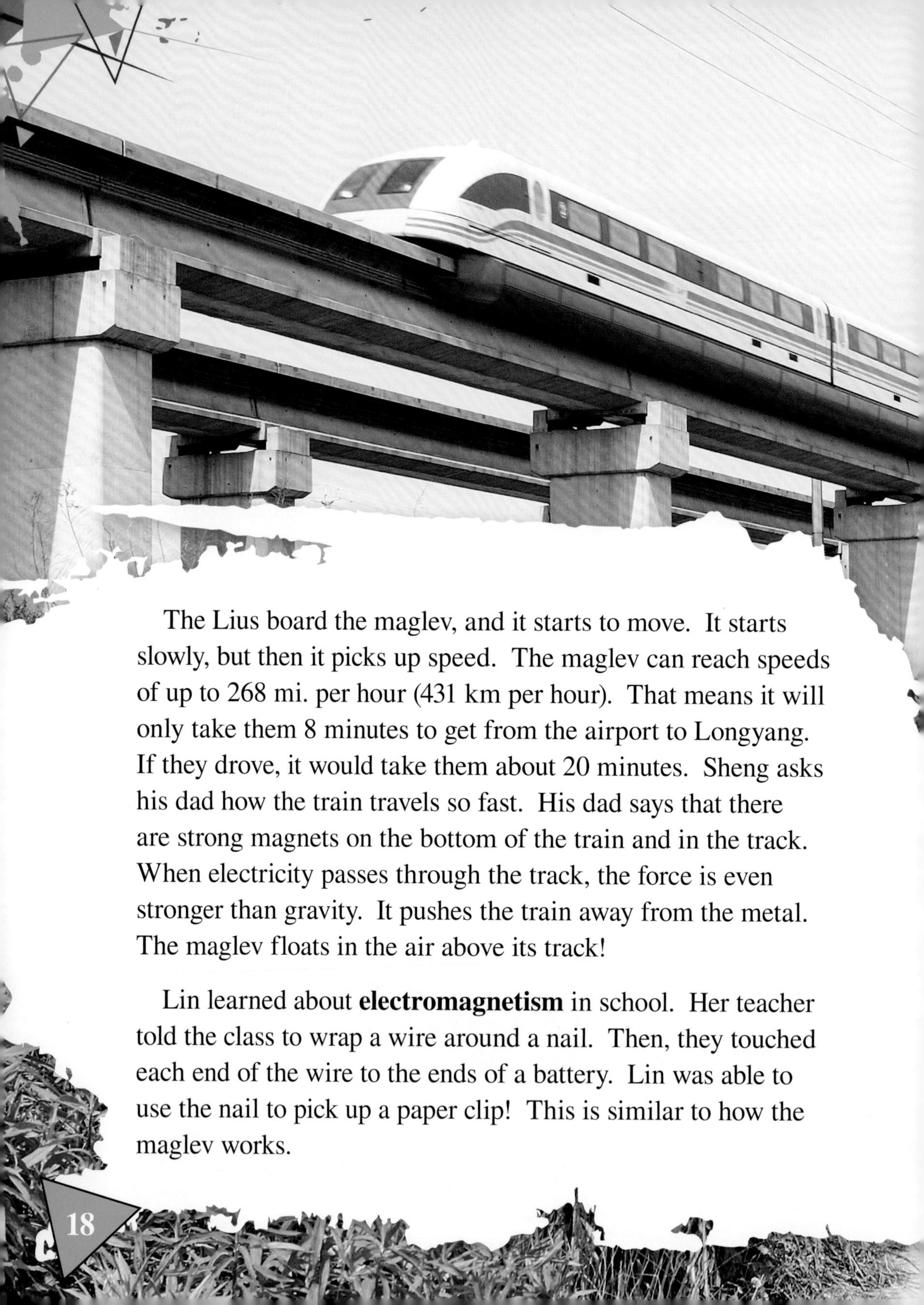

The Lius board the maglev, and it starts to move. It starts slowly, but then it picks up speed. The maglev can reach speeds of up to 268 mi. per hour (431 km per hour). That means it will only take them 8 minutes to get from the airport to Longyang. If they drove, it would take them about 20 minutes. Sheng asks his dad how the train travels so fast. His dad says that there are strong magnets on the bottom of the train and in the track. When electricity passes through the track, the force is even stronger than gravity. It pushes the train away from the metal. The maglev floats in the air above its track!

Lin learned about **electromagnetism** in school. Her teacher told the class to wrap a wire around a nail. Then, they touched each end of the wire to the ends of a battery. Lin was able to use the nail to pick up a paper clip! This is similar to how the maglev works.

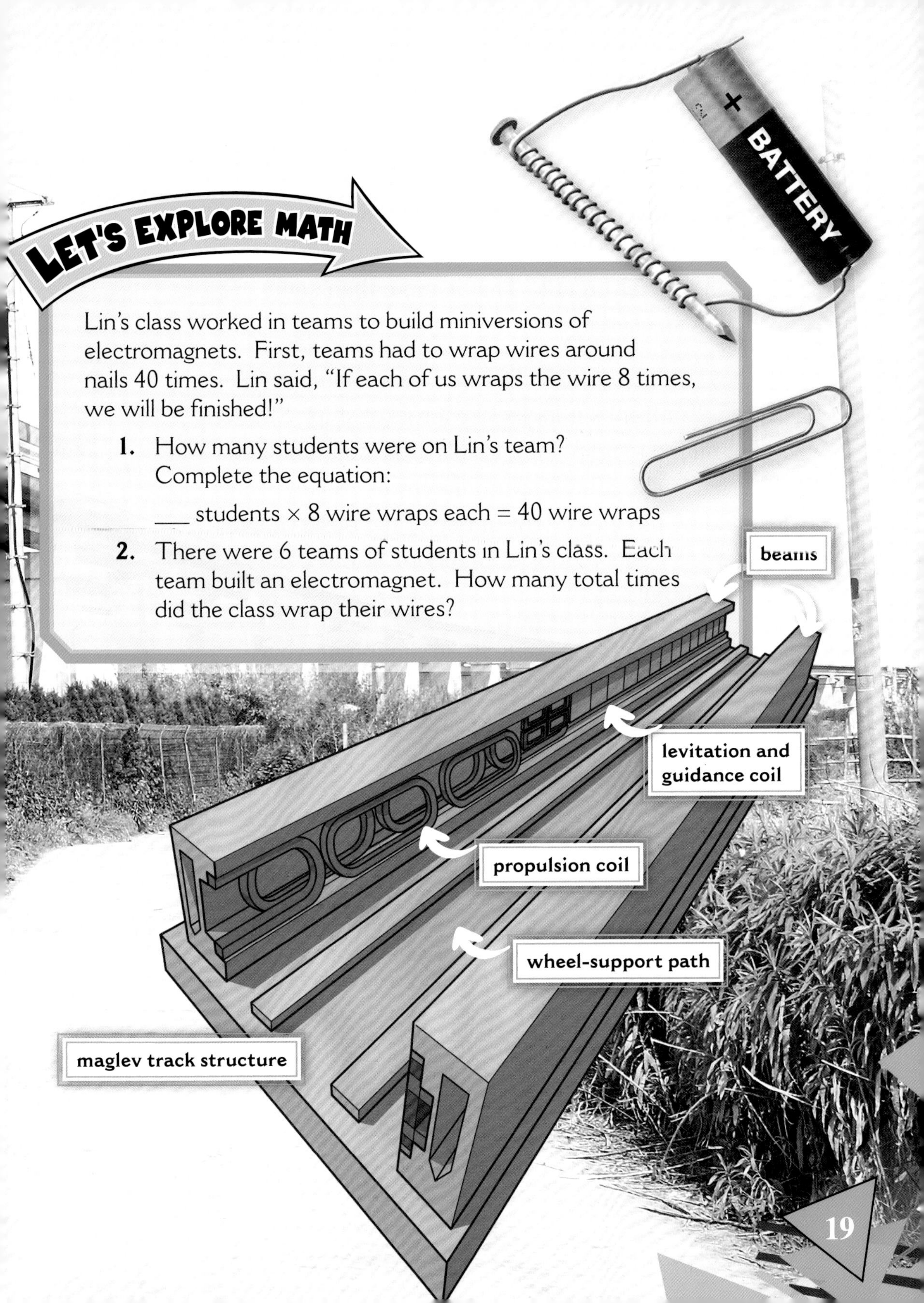

LET'S EXPLORE MATH

Lin's class worked in teams to build miniversions of electromagnets. First, teams had to wrap wires around nails 40 times. Lin said, "If each of us wraps the wire 8 times, we will be finished!"

1. How many students were on Lin's team? Complete the equation:

   ___ students × 8 wire wraps each = 40 wire wraps

2. There were 6 teams of students in Lin's class. Each team built an electromagnet. How many total times did the class wrap their wires?

Lin and Sheng look out the window of the maglev. They watch the city zoom by. They can see the Shanghai Tower in the distance. It is the tallest building in China. The swirling tower stands tall at 2,073 ft. (632 m) tall. That is more than eight airplanes stacked nose to tail!

They can also see the Oriental Pearl Radio & TV Tower. Lin thinks it looks like a rocket ship. She sees a sign on the maglev for a **revolving** restaurant at the tower. It is about halfway up the tower. Sheng wants to stand on the glass floor of one of the observation decks. He wants to look straight down to see the ground far below!

They arrive at Longyang Road Station in what seems like no time at all. Lin, Sheng, and their parents step off the train. They are ready to explore the sights and sounds of Shanghai!

Longyang Road Station
Shanghai Transrapid

Double-Decker Delight

Before the Lius can explore the city, they need to drop off their suitcases at the hotel. They hop on a bus, and Sheng looks around in awe. The bus has two levels! It is a double-decker bus. He and Lin want to sit on the top level. The top level does not have a roof, so there is a lot to see!

As they ride, Sheng and Lin look to the left and right to see all of the sights. The bus ride is not as fast as the maglev. Traveling on the busy city streets means the bus must make a lot of stops. The driver needs to obey traffic signals. And, he needs to watch out for **pedestrians**.

The bus brings them to the Shanghai World Financial Center. It is the second-tallest building in the city. It has offices, shops, and even a hotel on the 79th floor! Lin cannot believe they are staying here!

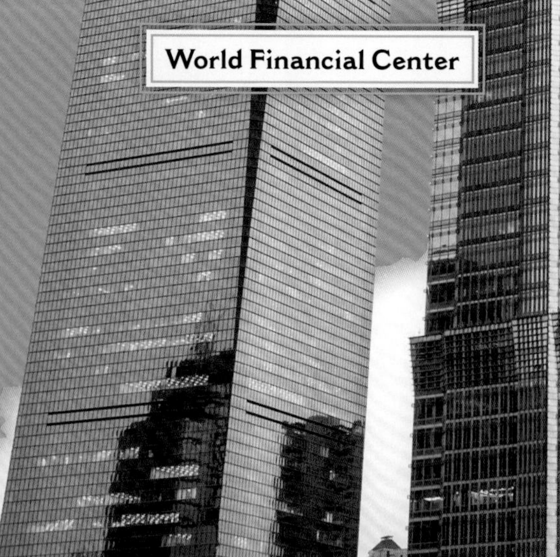

World Financial Center

Visitors to Shanghai see the sights from an open-top tour bus.

LET'S EXPLORE MATH

The double-decker bus makes 9 stops while the Lius are heading to the Shanghai World Financial Center.

1. At each stop, 6 passengers get off the bus. How many total passengers exit the bus?
2. At each stop, 7 passengers board the bus. How many new passengers board the bus?
3. Do more passengers exit the bus or board the bus? How many more?

Underground Travel

Now that they have settled in at their hotel, the family is ready for more fun. Next stop: family visit! The Lius walk to the nearest subway station and head down a long set of stairs. The subway is a system of trains that go all over the city. Shanghai's subway system is considered the longest single-system route in the world.

While waiting for the train, Sheng sees tall glass walls along the edges of the platform. His mother tells him that these walls block the noise of the trains.

Sheng covers his ears. His mother was not kidding when she said trains were loud! Unlike the maglev, subway trains use metal wheels that travel along metal tracks. This creates noise. To come to a stop, brakes have to squeeze the tracks. This results in a force called **friction**. It slows the train. It makes noise, too. Sheng prefers the floating maglev. It was fast, smooth, and *quiet*! But when Sheng looks at his sister, Lin is smiling. She thinks the subway feels like a roller coaster ride! She wishes she could ride the subway all day!

LET'S EXPLORE MATH

A short one-way ride on Shanghai's subway costs 3 **yuan** per person.

1. How much does the Liu family pay for 4 people to ride the subway?
2. A 24-hour subway pass costs 18 yuan per person. How many times more expensive is this pass than a one-way trip?

a subway station in Shanghai

Los Angeles, United States

Cancún, Mexico

Where Will You Go?

The Burkes and Lius all traveled to faraway places. They saw amazing things. A giant crater challenged the Burkes's hiking skills. Soaring skyscrapers wowed the Lius. Airplanes helped them travel far distances in short amounts of time. A helicopter and a bus helped them explore new areas. The maglev and subway made getting around a breeze.

Where do you want to go? Do you want to visit a tropical island? Or, is a city more your style? Maybe you would like to stay close to home. Exploring what your town has to offer can be fun, too! The next time it is your turn to travel, near or far, remember that the journey there is part of the fun!

Banff National Park in Canada

Problem Solving

The Burkes and Lius went on family vacations. But some people like to travel in large groups. Often, travel agents help these groups make arrangements. They buy tickets and book seats on planes, trains, and buses. They reserve rooms at hotels and tables at restaurants.

Kaya, a travel agent, is booking a trip for a group of 100 people. The group will need several forms of transportation during the trip. Kaya needs to carefully plan for the group's needs.

1. Complete the plan for each method of transportation. Remember, there are 100 people in the tour group.

   a. airplane
   ________ rows, 5 seats in each row

   b. double-decker bus
   2 decks, ________ passengers on each deck

   c. subway
   10 cars, ________ passengers in each car

   d. helicopter
   ________ helicopters, 4 passengers in each helicopter

2. Write a multiplication equation for each method of transportation to prove that each plan will work.

Small World
TRAVEL AGENCY
Travel Agent: Kaya Tripper
Traveler Information
Traveler Name
Date of Birth
www.London-CityTour.com
WiFi
ON
OFF
TICKETS
City Tour
LONDON

Glossary

aerial—seen from above

conveyor belt—a long strip of material that carries objects from one place to another

drag—resistance force that pulls things down

electromagnetism—magnetism that comes from a current of electricity

friction—force that causes a moving object to slow down when it touches another object

forces—pushes or pulls on objects

gravity—a force that acts between objects, pulling one toward the other

intercom—a system that allows a person speaking into a microphone to be heard in a different location

levitation—the act of rising into the air

lift—force that opposes gravity and is generated by motion that pushes things up

pedestrians—people who are walking

revolving—spinning around a center point

rotors—parts of a machine that move around a center point

switchback—a zigzag trail for climbing a steep hill

thrust—force that pushes things forward

yuan—the basic unit of money used in China

Index

Answer Key

Let's Explore Math

page 7:

1. 24 pieces of luggage
2. 3 bags per person

page 11:

1. 30 mi. wide
2. 10 mi. wide

page 15:

1. 40 min.
2. 60 min.

page 19:

1. 5
2. 240 wire wraps

page 23:

1. 54 passengers
2. 63 passengers
3. More passengers boarded the bus; 9 more

page 25:

1. 12 yuan
2. 6 times more expensive

Problem Solving

1. **a.** 20
   b. 50
   c. 10
   d. 25
2. $20 \times 5 = 100$; $2 \times 50 = 100$; $10 \times 10 = 100$; $25 \times 4 = 100$